The Amazing Race: The Atlantic Slave Trade Through the Pages of Book Art

-

A Traveling Exhibition

Objects designed and created by Book Artist

Martha H. Edgerton

Baltimore, Maryland

2016

The Artist

After a 35-year career in the preservation field, conserving rare library materials at prestigious educational institutions in the mid-Atlantic region, Martha Edgerton made the transition from book and paper conservation to book art. She is the creator of the traveling exhibition entitled "The Amazing Race: The Atlantic Slave Trade through the Pages of Book Art" (TARBAE).

Exhibit production had been a major part of Edgerton's duties throughout her preservation career. She uses those skills combined with her knowledge of various techniques used in bookbinding and the visual arts to create the unique objects for her traveling exhibition.

TARBAE premiered at the Enoch Pratt Free Library, Baltimore, Maryland, February 2015. From there, the exhibit (or select items from the exhibit) appeared at the Reginald F. Lewis Museum and other Maryland institutions. It has received attention from institutions and individuals across the United States. Local Maryland schools and libraries use it as a teaching tool for general and specific projects. The main piece of TARBAE, entitled "I Was Once Lost," won first prize in the 2017 Juried Members' Exhibition at the Pyramid Atlantic Art Center (Hyattsville, Maryland).

Edgerton's training, certification, and educational background includes: a five-year apprenticeship program in book and paper conservation/preservation at the Johns Hopkins University, a one-year internship in rare book and paper conservation/preservation at the Library of Congress, as well as a BS degree in Interdisciplinary Studies from the Johns Hopkins University.

This Catalog

This catalog does not show every object in the exhibit and is not expected to provide the full experience of seeing the objects in person. However Edgerton hopes that it will serve as a momento for those who have seen it and as an invitation to those who have yet to see it. It can also be used as a teaching tool for discussion of this important aspect of American history as well as the craft of book art.

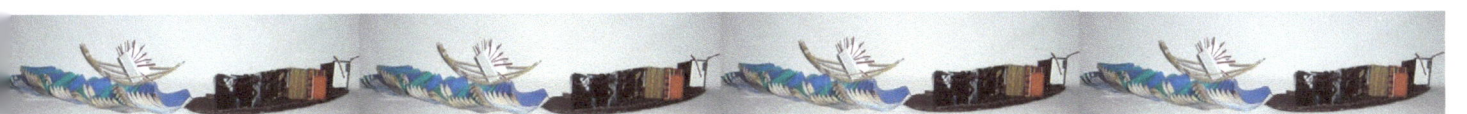

THE EXHIBITION

Europeans had been involved in trade with Africa extensively before the transatlantic slave trade. They sought spices, salt, gold, ivory, and more. What began as a quest for these materials led to the trade of black Africans. The title of this exhibit, *The Amazing Race*, exemplifies the extraordinary strength, courage, and grace of the African people and their descendants who survived this African diaspora to become valuable, productive citizens of the Americas. The subtitle, *The Atlantic Slave Trade through the Pages of Book Art,* informs the viewer of the topic (slavery) and names the unique art form (book art). In the form of traditional and contemporary bookmaking and paper crafting, *The Amazing Race* exhibition is designed to chronicle certain aspects of the Atlantic slave experience from its beginnings in African to its early years in the Americas.

The exhibit is divided into four sections. The first is about *capture,* beginning with representations of everyday African life before and during capture. The second section is about the *middle passage,* with some depictions of key players during the transport phase of slavery. The third is about *being a slave*, highlighting labor and products. The fourth is about *becoming African American*—with emphasis on the struggles they faced in gaining freedom.

Each uniquely hand-made art object is either made from scratch or by the alteration of an existing book and paper object.

Section I: Capture

The horrific capturing, trading, and transporting of Africans for enslavement in the Americas entailed horrible acts of violence, abduction, mutilation, family separation, killing and more.

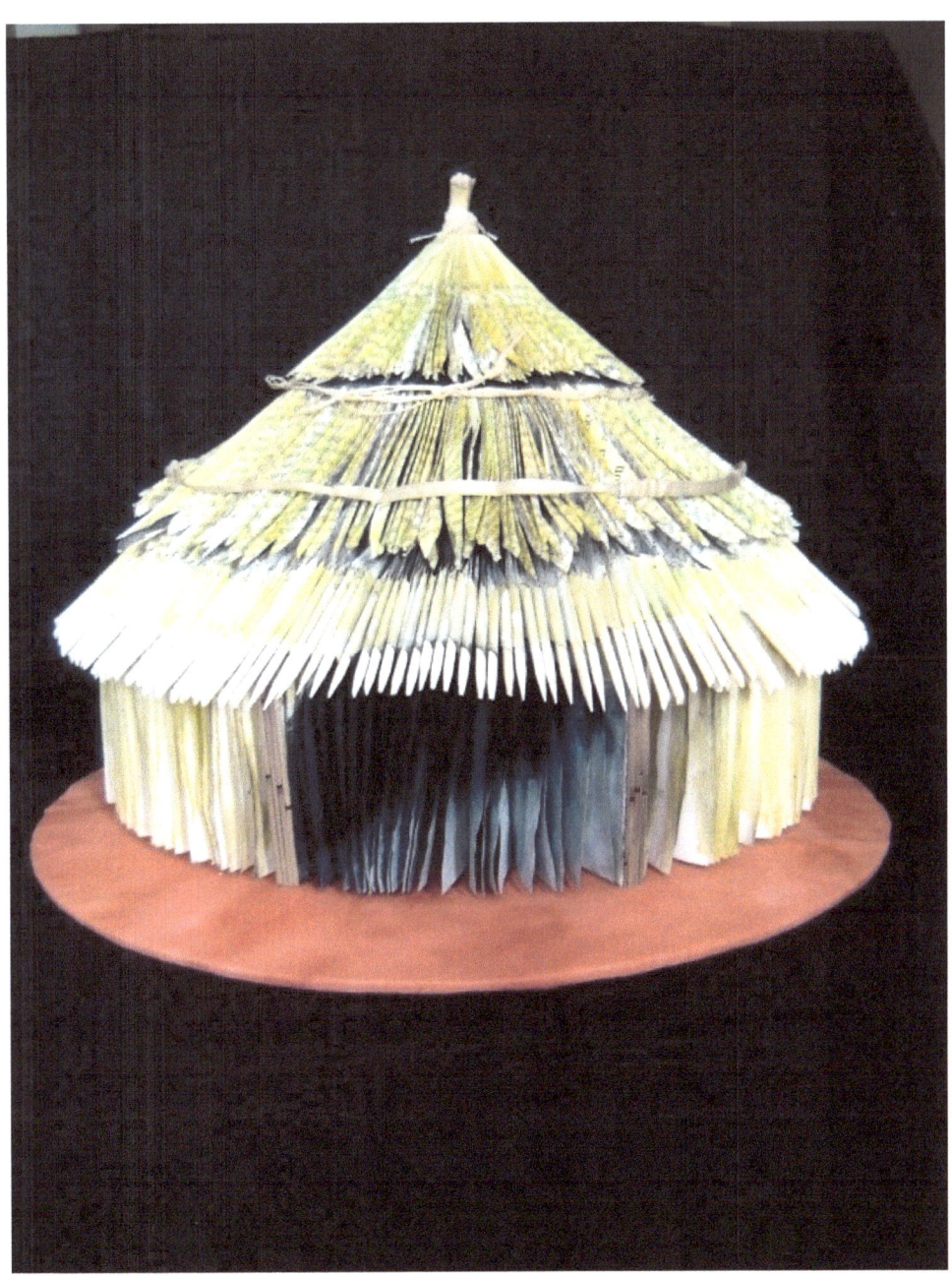

Motherland I

Martha Edgerton. 2013.

An *altered book* depicts a traditional African hut, a place some Africans called home before capture—symbolizing peace and family unity before capture.

29cm(H) x 36cm(W)

Mixed media: paper, cloth, glue, straw twine, acrylic paint

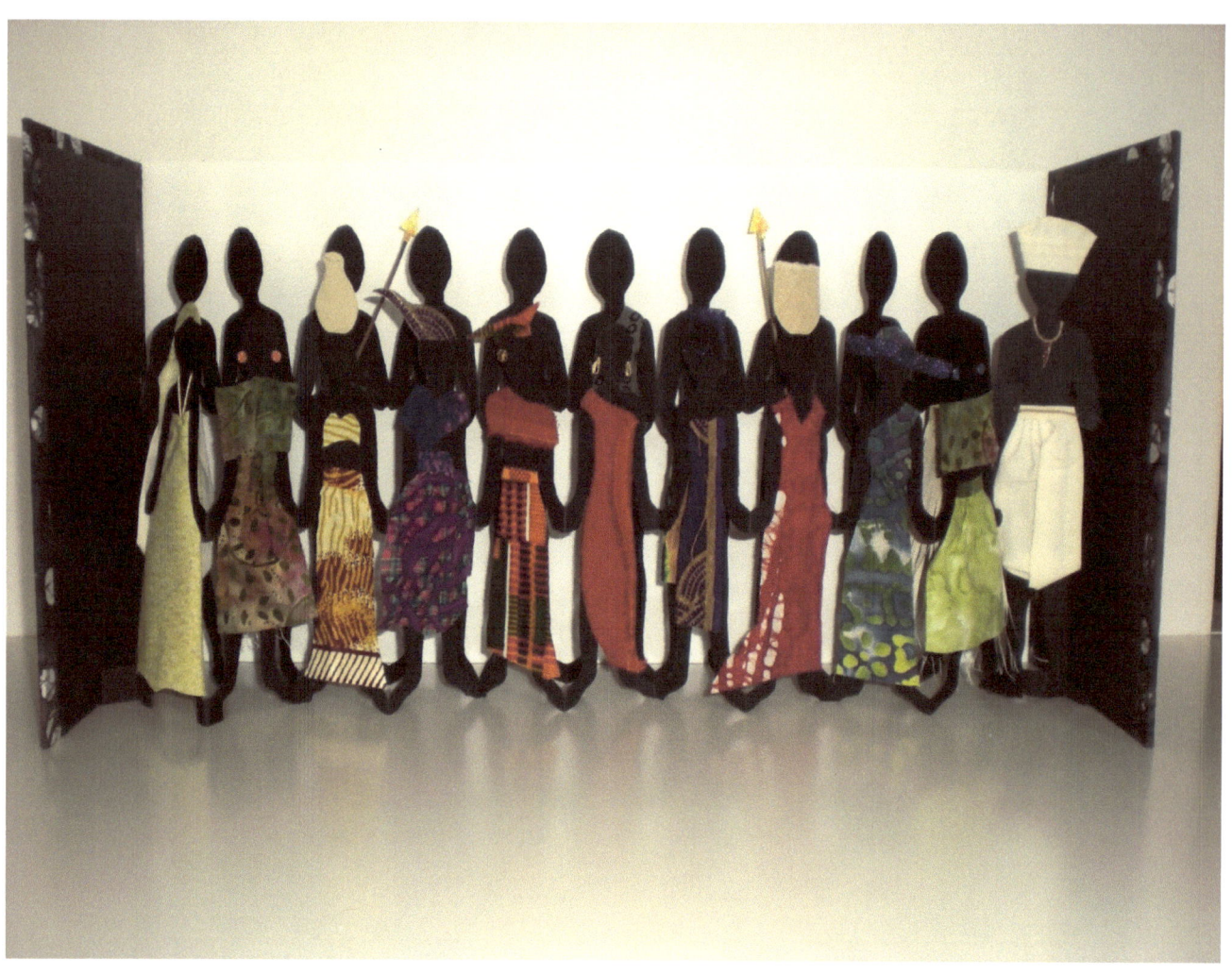

Traded Spices II

Martha Edgerton. 2013.

An *accordion cloth binding* displaying Africans in their various roles and statuses before capture: workers, hunters, gatherers, royalty, mothers, fathers, etc.

26cm(H) x 52cm(W—open) x 16.5cm(D)

Mixed media: fabric, binders board, cloth, glue, paper, wooden sticks, metal

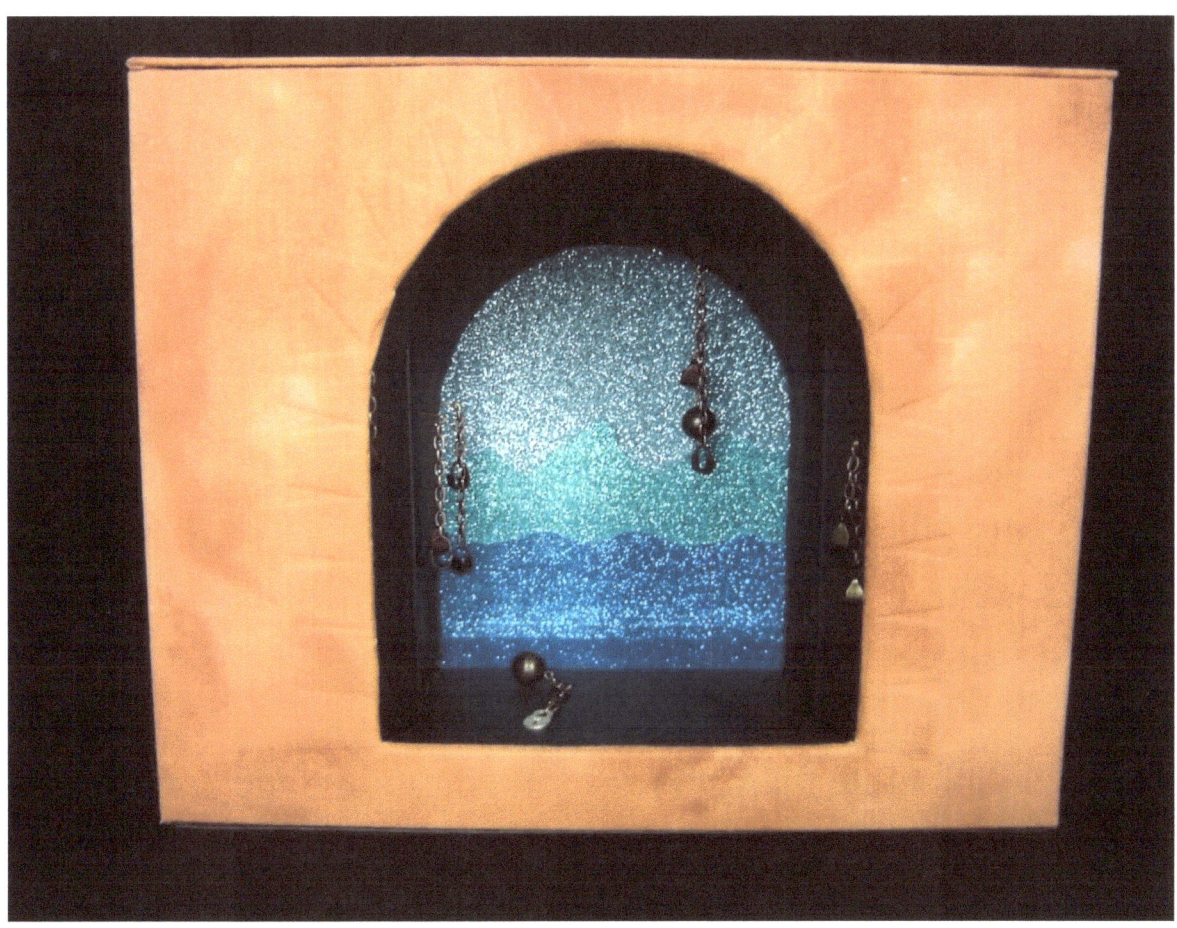

Return No More

Martha Edgerton. 2013.

A **theater box** symbolizes the "Door of No Return," a temporary holding place for captured Africans until their transport across the Atlantic Ocean to the Americas.

23cm(H) x 28.7cm(W) x 20cm(D)

mixed media: cloth, binders board, glue, metal, paper, mat board

Section II: Middle Passage

The Middle Passage, the forced transoceanic journey for African slaves, was a continuation of the horror. During this phase of slavery, Africans were beaten, forced-fed, and made to do other activities unfamiliar to themselves. Many knew nothing about their destinations or future. Many died from disease, mistreatment, and some even committed suicide. Some attempted to liberate themselves through mutiny and some were successful.

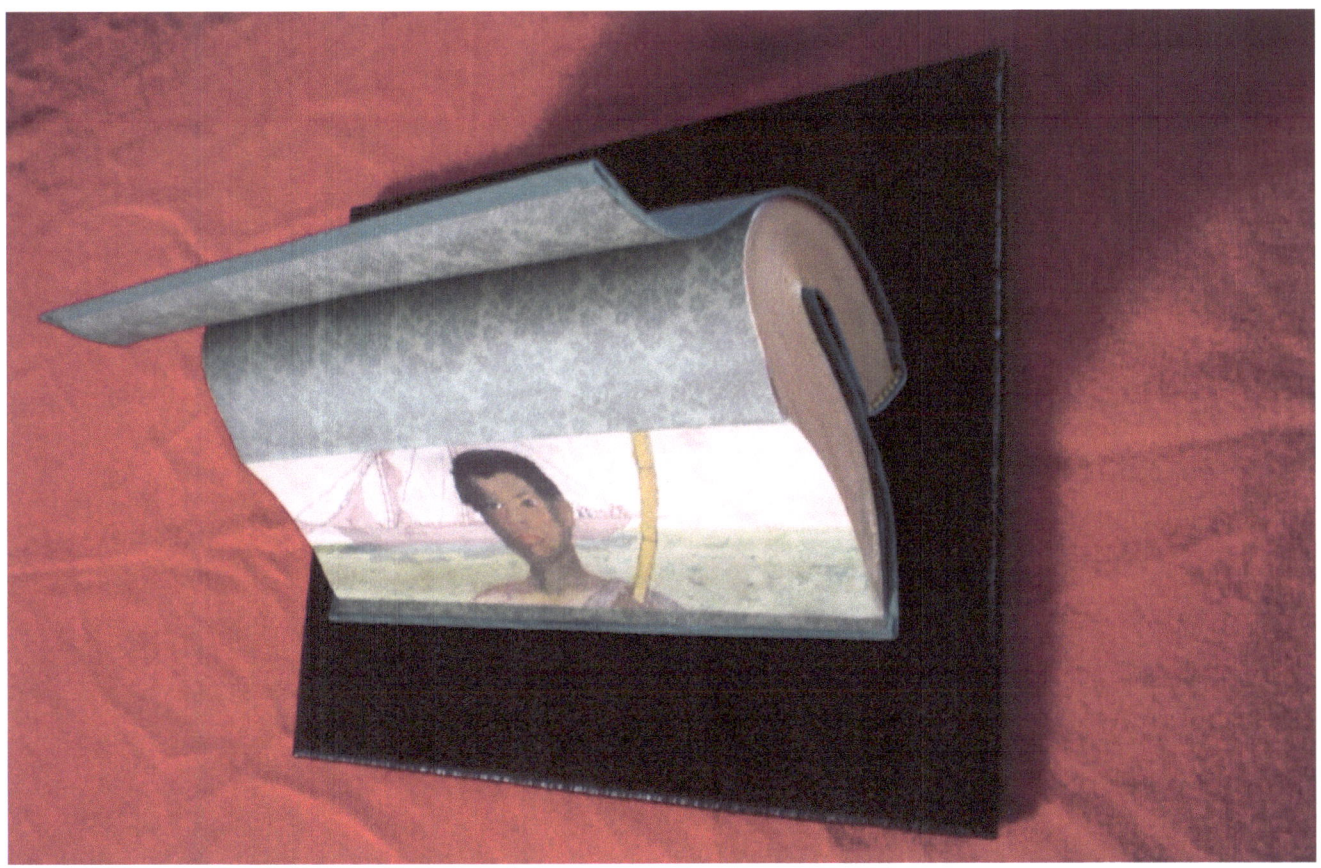

Cinque I

Martha Edgerton. 2006.

An ***altered cloth binding*** with a fore-edge painting depicts the famous Cinque in his homeland before captivity.

23.5cm(H) x 16cm(W) x 7cm(D)

Mixed media: paper, glue, book cloth, thread, metal posts, water color pigment, binders board, cloth

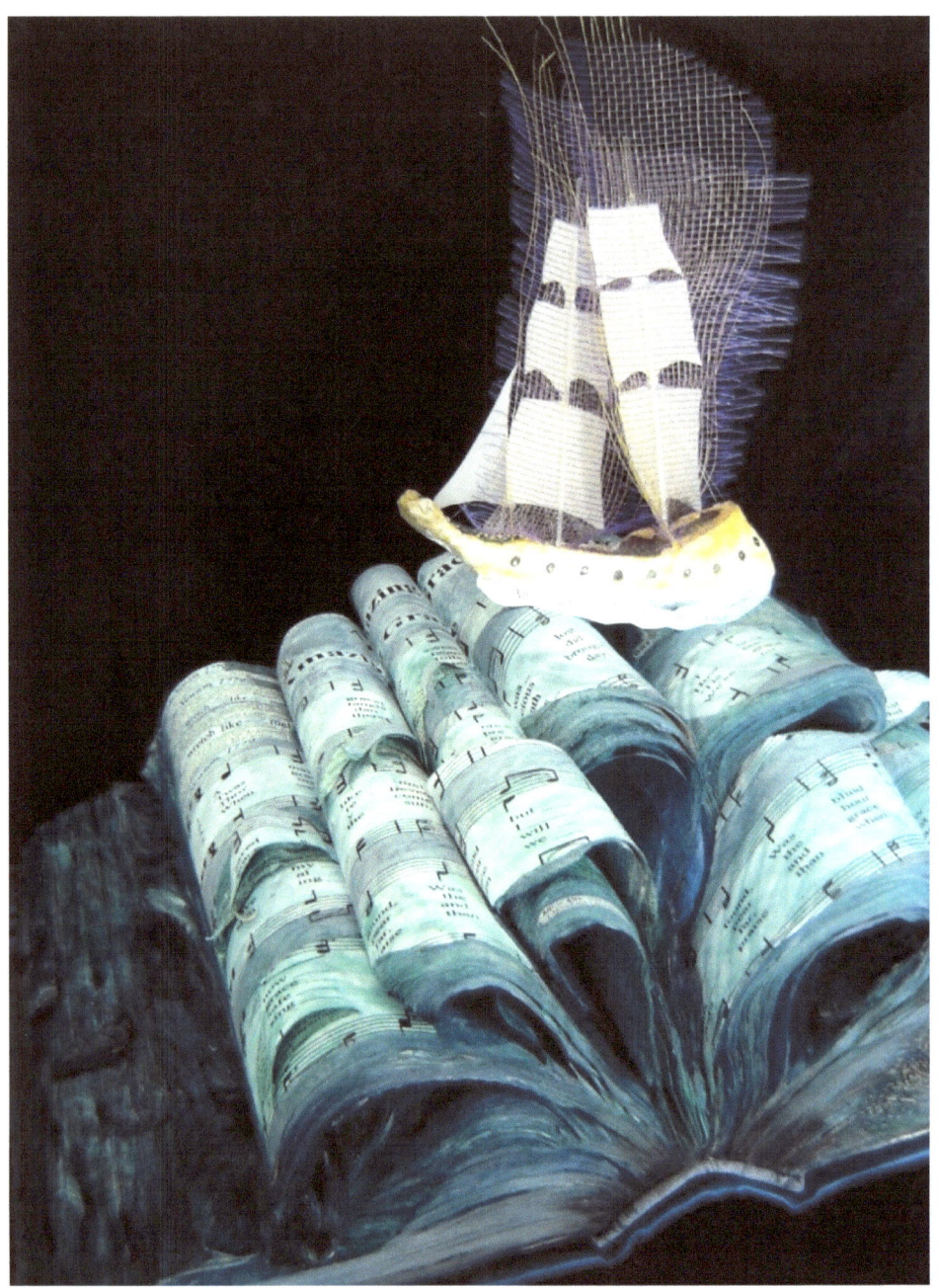

I Was Once Lost

Martha Edgerton. 2011.

An ***altered book*** portrays a middle passage ocean scene and a connection to Captain John Newton's redemption song "Amazing Grace."

40cm(H) x 28.5cm(D) x 50cm(W)

Mixed media: cloth, binders board, glue, paper, nylon thread/mesh, water and acrylic pigments

Section III: To Be a Slave

The enslaved Africans were stripped of their own African identities (cultures, family connections, names, skills, languages, and more) and forced to adapt to the identity assigned by their owner(s). Slave owners considered their slaves to be less than human. Owners handled and mishandled (traded, sold, relocated, punished, and even destroyed) their slaves like they did any other traded commodity—with no regard for human dignity. Slaves were forced to work from sun up to sun down usually seven days a week with no monetary rewards for their labor. During the colonial period, prominent religious groups saw reasons to educate the slaves: conversion and reading scriptures—which allowed for another form of control. Slaves were taught and allowed to read and draw, but not to write; even so, some slaves did learn to write. As slave owners realized and feared the power of slave literacy—slave to slave communication, escape via forged documents (passes, freedom papers, etc.), access to and enticement of abolitionist materials, etc.—they saw the need to prohibit slave education. In the early 1700s, the U.S. began to established slave codes to make it illegal to teach slaves to read and write. Slaves had no freedoms; they were imprisoned where they lived.

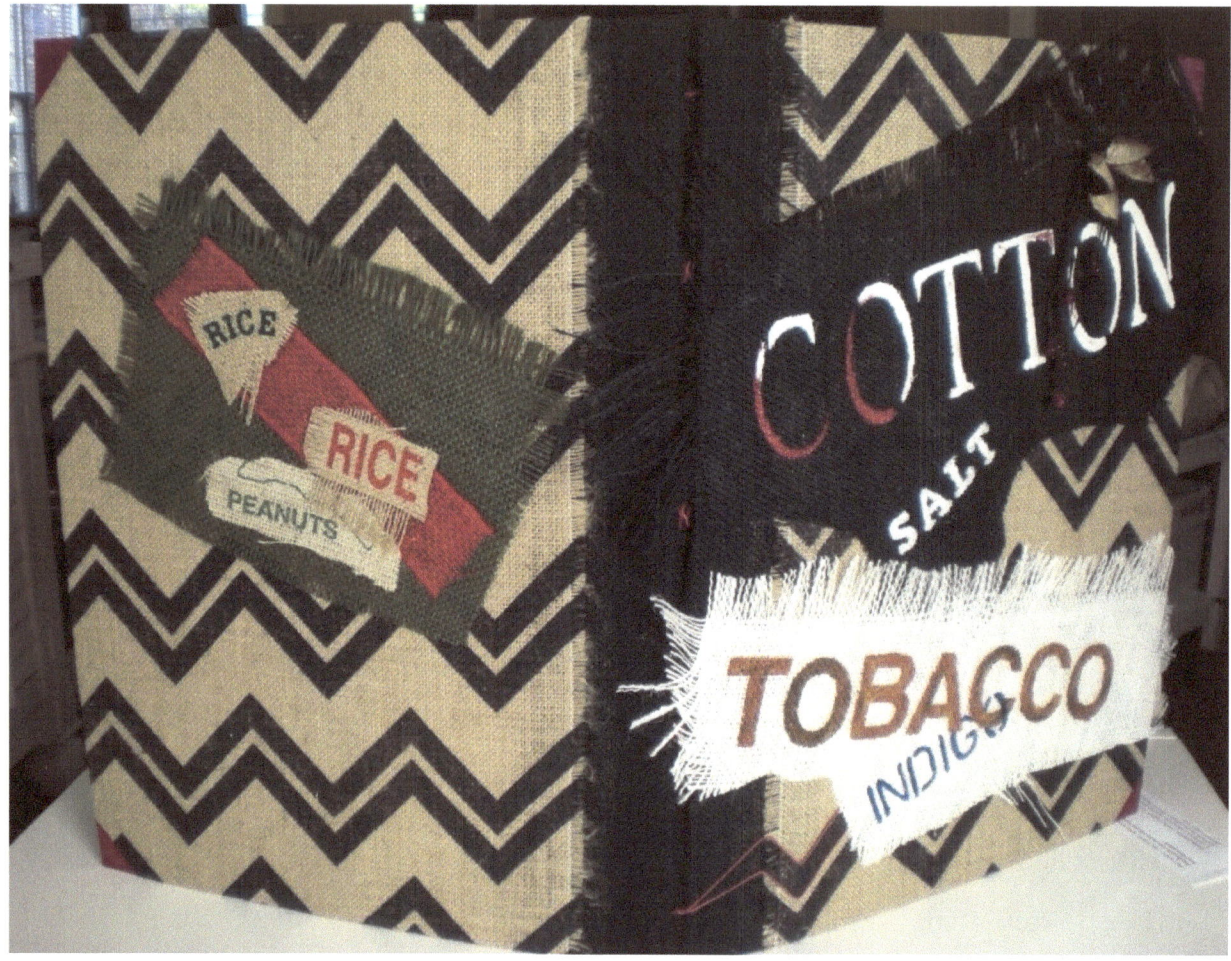

Fruits of Our Labor IV (outside cover)

Martha Edgerton. 2013.

A ***cloth binding*** and its pages express through words and illustrations the major and minor products of slave labor throughout the Americas: cotton, tobacco, rice, indigo, sugar, peanuts, and more. The red glass beads represent the blood, sweat, and tears shed by the slave laborers.

51.5 cm (H) x 39 cm (W) x 2.0 (D)

Mixed media: burlap, binders board, leather, paper, glue, pigments, beads, and thread

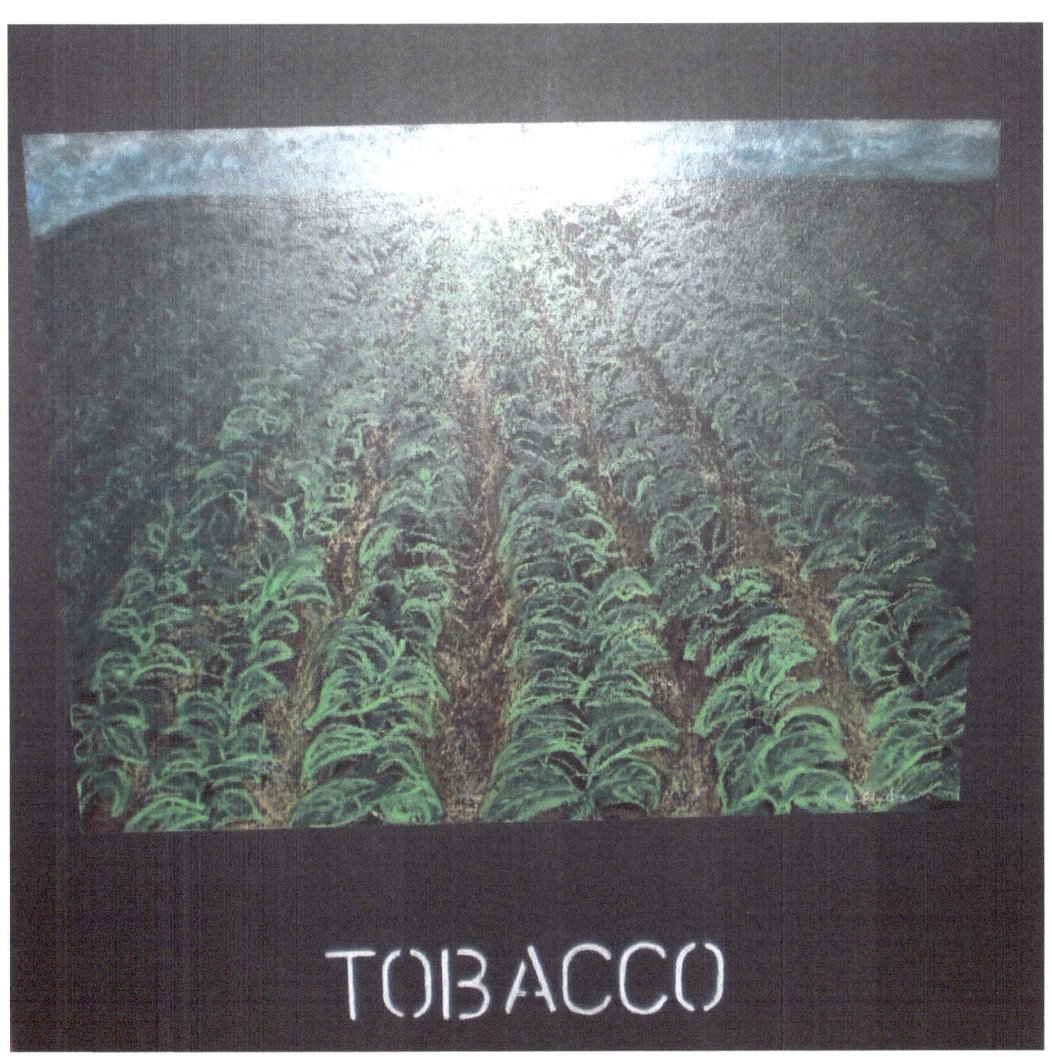

Fruits of Our Labor IV (an inside page)

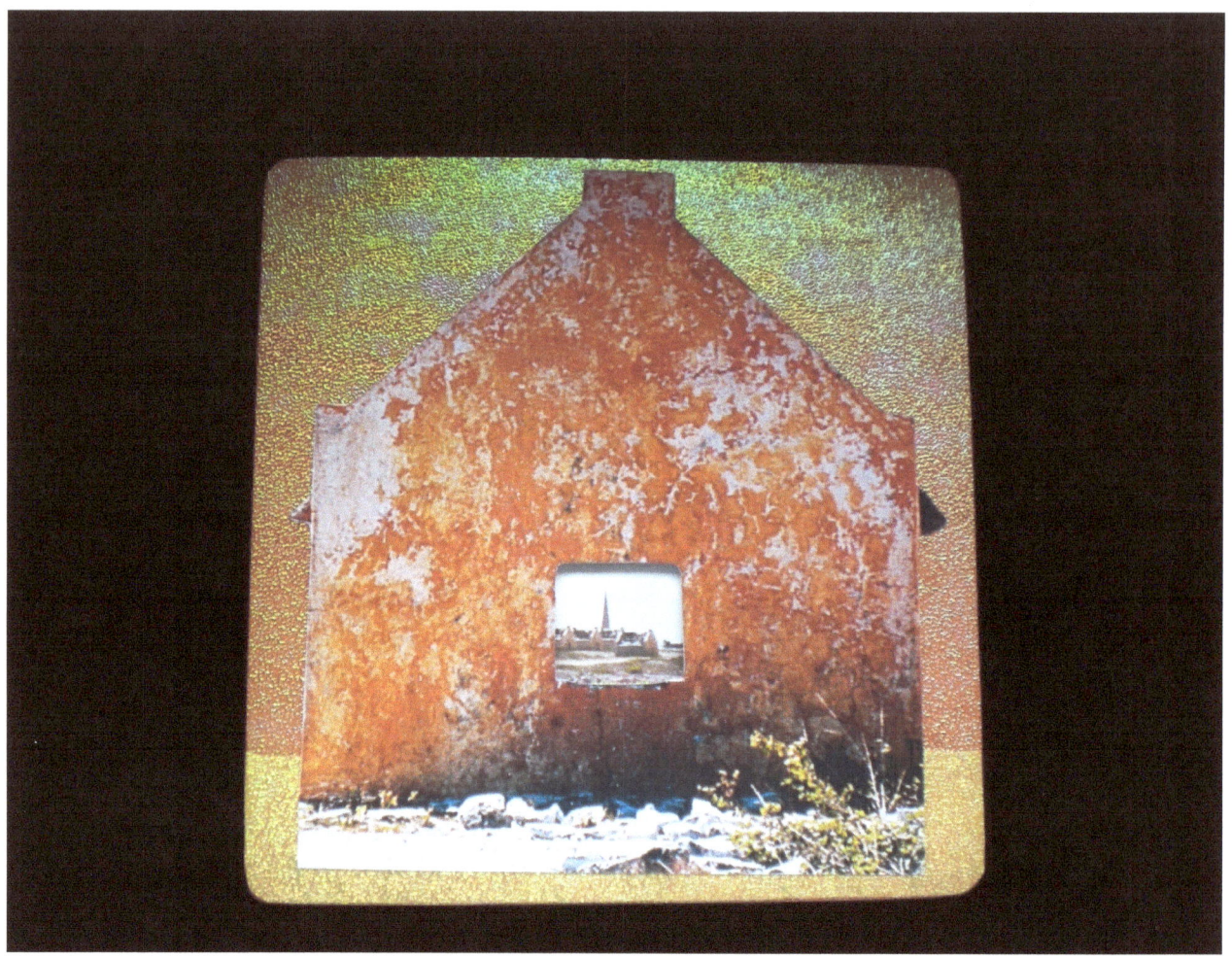

Fruits of Our Labor III (pictured here is the cover)

Martha Edgerton. 2013.

An ***accordion binding*** depicts living quarters of the first African slaves in Bonaire. The slaves built these huts and other structures. They were forced to work cutting dyewood, cultivating maize and harvesting solar salt at the salt pans.

20cm(H) x 20cm/125cm displayed(L)

Mixed media: glue, wooden boards, paper, pigments

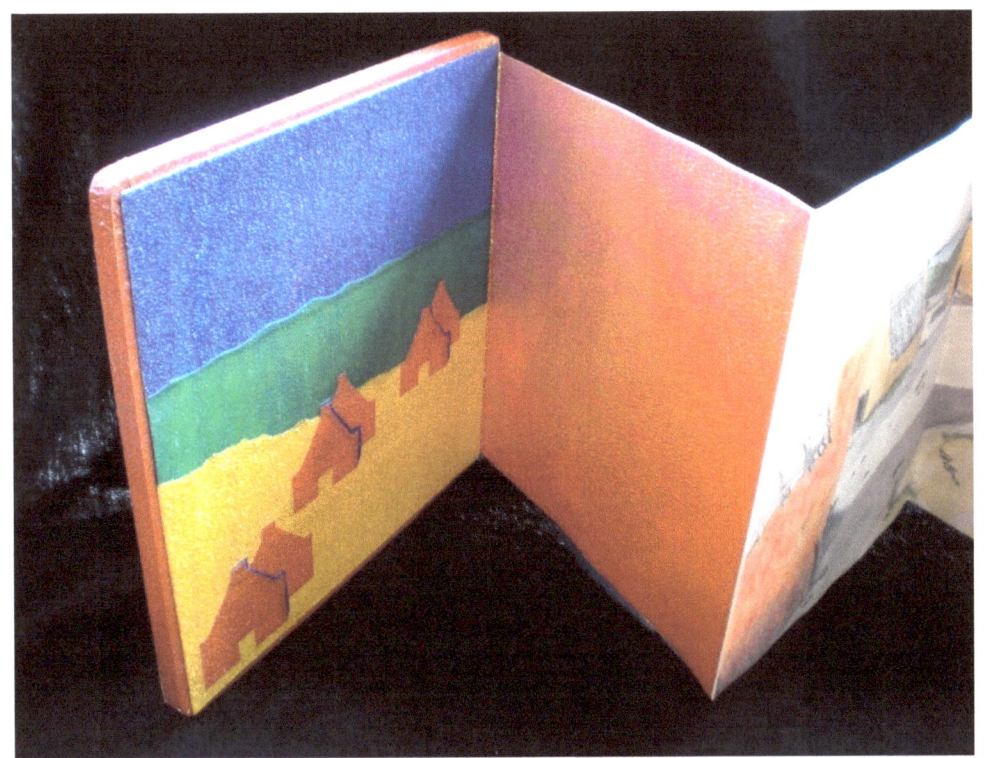

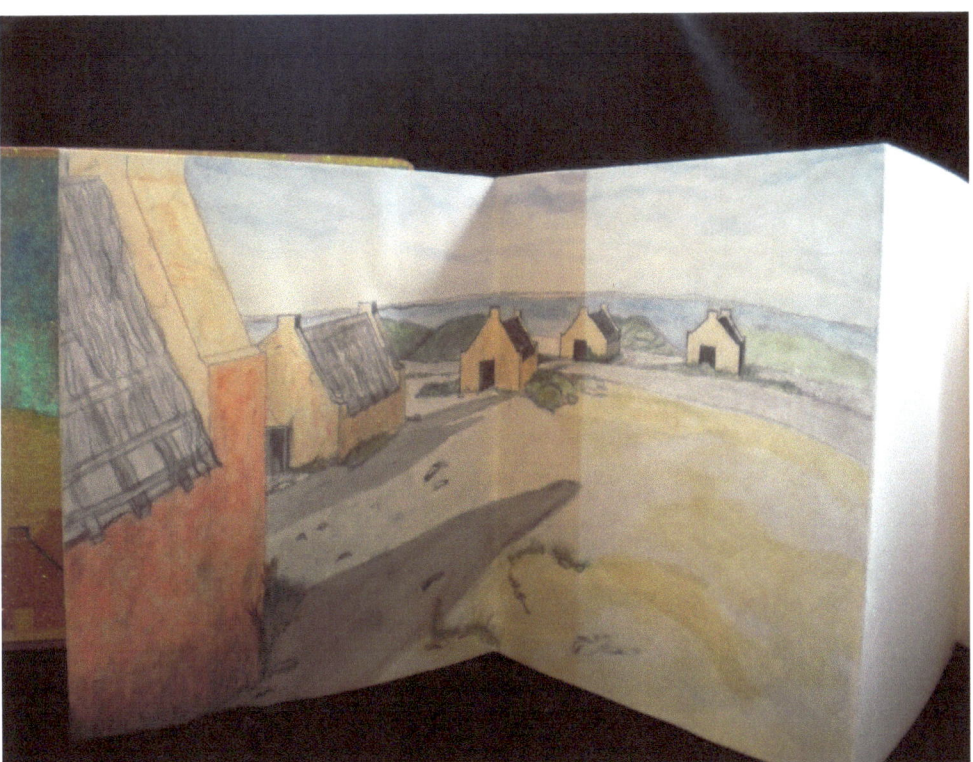

Fruits of Our Labor III (inside pages)

Section IV: Becoming African American

Slaves contemplated freedom from the moment they were enslaved in Africa to the time that they became chattel in the Americas. Once they were freed of the chains that bound them, the world was forced to acknowledge their powers, abilities, and humanity.

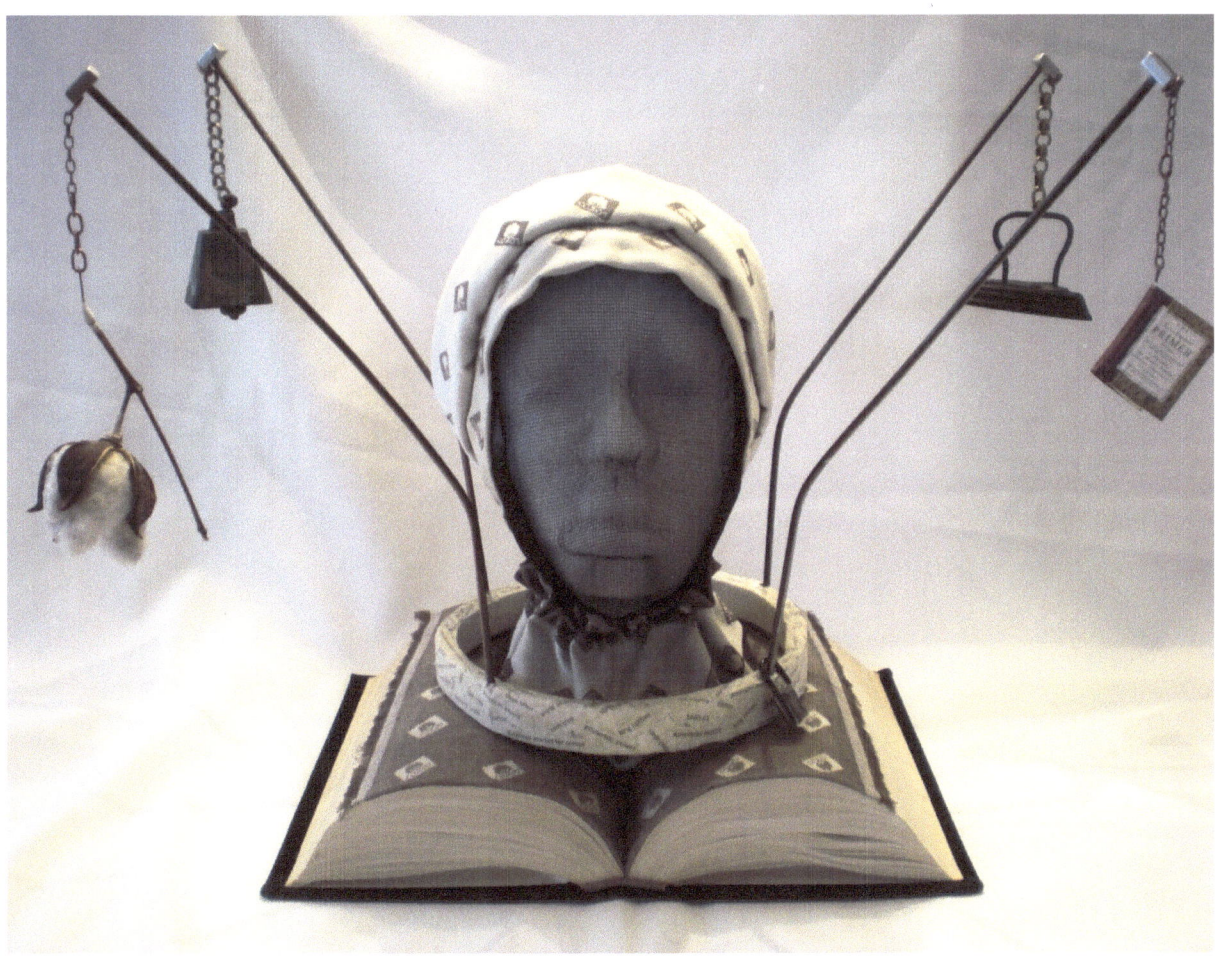

Tasting Freedom

Martha Edgerton. 2013.

An ***altered book*** illustrates policies and practices designed to forever keep the slaves locked in bondage and stagnation; however, the slaves continued to seek freedom. This device, a slave collar with bells, is typical of restraining instruments used to prevent people from running away. The meshed faces (one black, one white) represents the oppressed and the oppressor.

39cm(H) x 36cm(W) x 29cm(D)

Mixed media: binders board, paper, cloth, metal, fabric, wire mesh, Styrofoam pigments, thread, glue

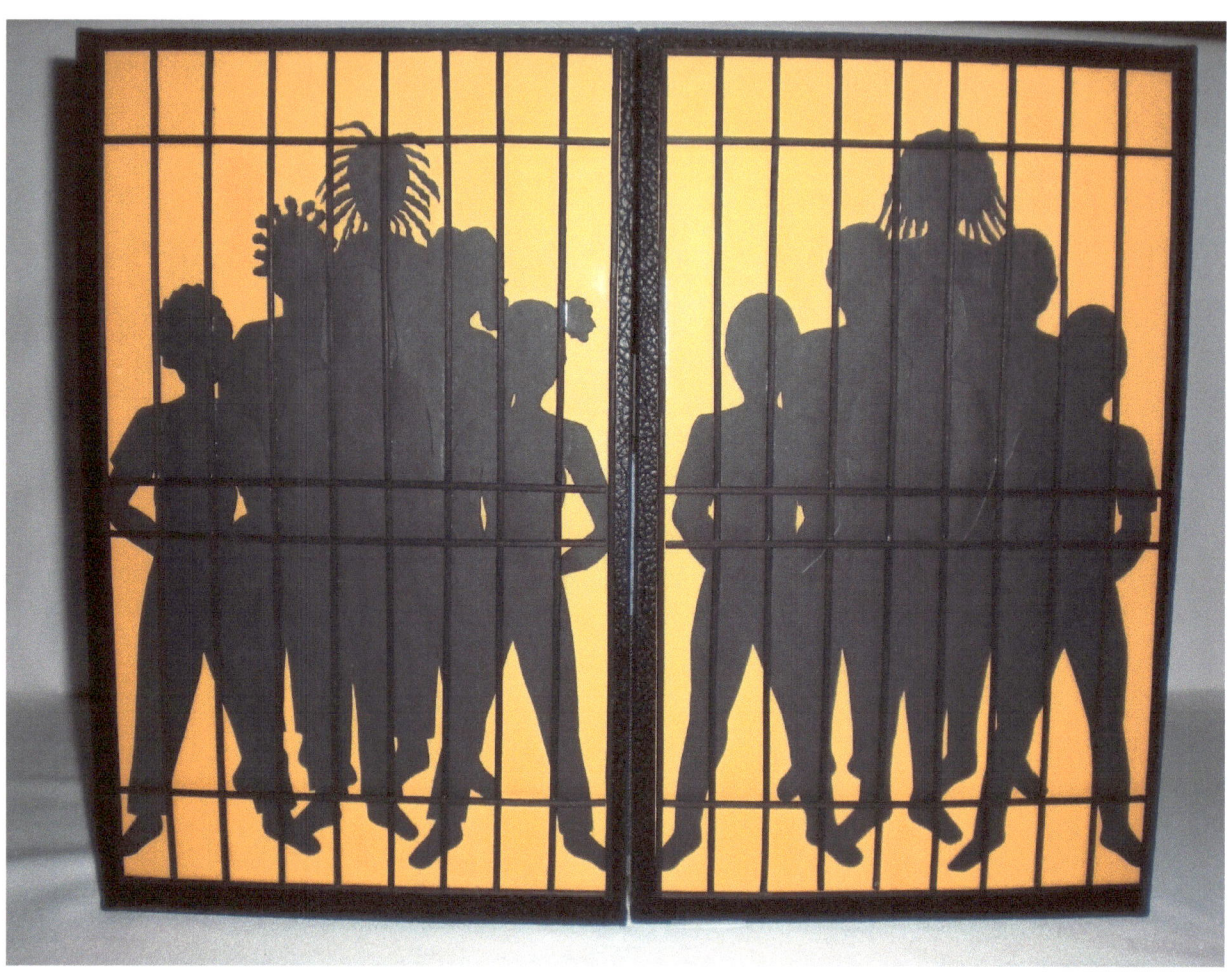

Then and Now (outside cover)

Martha Edgerton. 2013.

A ***pop-out accordion binding*** that depicts the state of mass incarceration of blacks in America during the slave era and today.

Mixed media: Mylar (polyester film), pigments (water colors), wood, paper, fabric, glue, binders board, double side tape

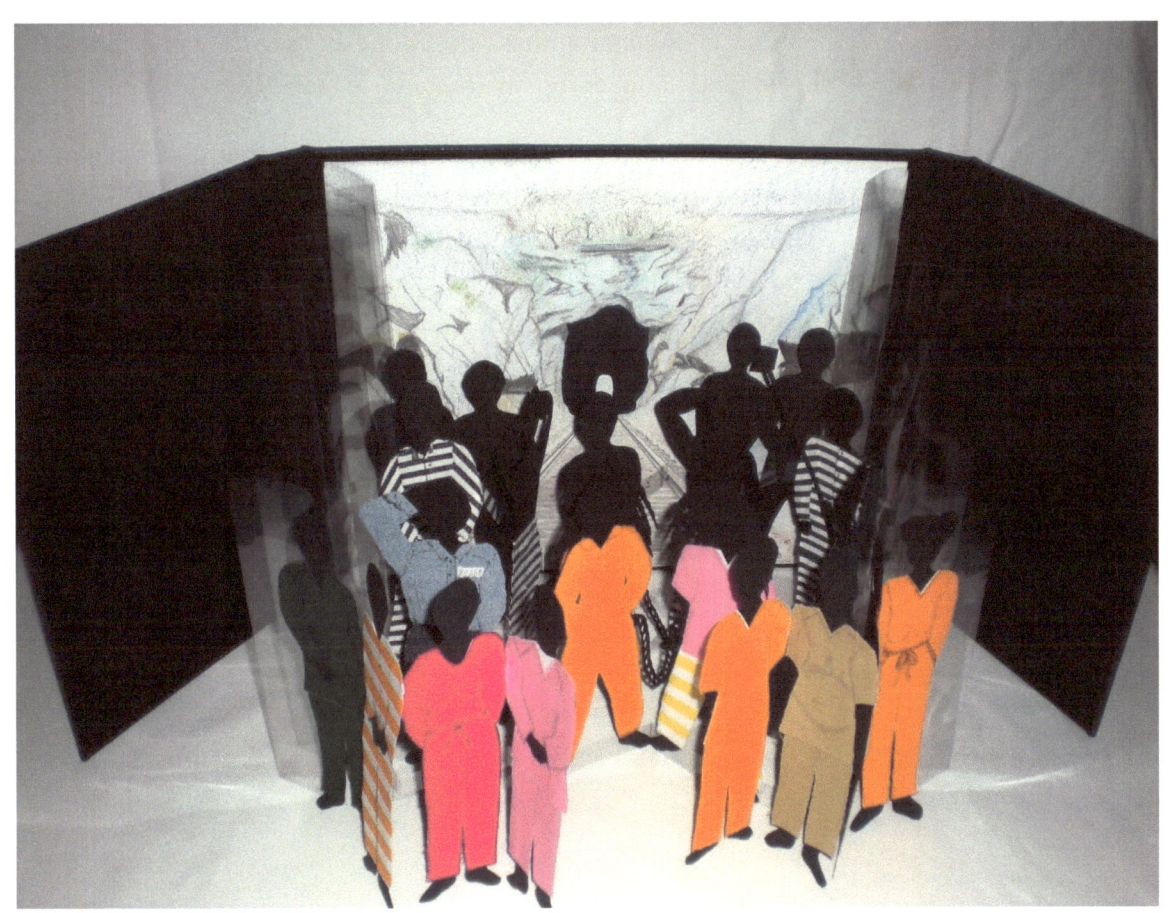

Then and Now (inside)

Acknowlegements from the Artist

For me, one of the most exciting aspects of creating this exhibition has been the opportunity to learn more about the topic of slavery and about early American history in general.

The generous help of many others contributed to bringing my vision to successful completion. To my dear family and friends (too numerous to name here) who assisted and supported me emotionally and physically I want to say, I know you did it out of love. Words cannot explain how truly thankful I am to have you in my life and I love you back! You know who you are: listeners/advisors, mentors, proof-readers, book artist friend/co-exhibitor and other bookmakers, the cabinet maker, the transporter, the cake maker, sounding-boards, the photographer, object models, and cheer-leaders.

I am deeply indebted to all library staff of the Enoch Pratt *free* Library (EPFL) who provided the services that gave this exhibition its wonderful start, especially those of the following departments: Collectons Management- Preservation/Bindery Unit, Facilitities, Programs and Publications, Security, Special Collections, and the Resource Center. A very special thanks to Dr. Carla Hayden (former CEO of EPFL, now the Librarian of Congress) for her stamp of approval and wonderful remarks.

Thank you to the staff of the Reginald F. Lewis Museum for your generous and most helpful advice, and for giving the exhibit a support and an exposure that widened its impact.

To inquire about hosting this exhibition, please contact the artist via her website:

http://medgerton53.wixsite.com/tarbae-book-art

www.ingramcontent.com/pod-product-compliance
Lightning Source LLC
Chambersburg PA
CBHW050439180526
45159CB00006B/2593